MW00976617

Simple Tips for

Simple

Living

for Teens

New Leaf Press

First Printing: March 2004

Cover by Left Coast Design, Portland, OR
Interior design by Brent Spurlock
Edited by Jim Fletcher and Roger Howerton

ISBN: 0-89221-573-9
Library of Congress Catalog Card Number: 2003116023

Please visit our web site for more great titles:
www.newleafpress.net

New Leaf Press

A special gift for you

To

_____

From

_____

1

Each day, **make time for quiet time**.
Relax and meditate on what you need
to do that day, and don't let worry
overtake you.

Renewal and restoration are not luxuries. They are essentials.
Being alone and resting for a while is not selfish. It is Christlike.

– Charles Swindoll

And the LORD gave them rest round about.
– Joshua 21:44

I will meditate in thy precepts, and have respect unto thy ways.
– Psalm 119:15

2

Don't Be Bullied!

Even if you're scared, try to look brave. Take slow deep breaths and tell yourself, "I can handle this."

Hang out with others. Being alone attracts bullies.

Tell an adult and ask for help. This is not tattling. You have a legitimate right to seek help.[1]

My defense is of God, which saveth the upright in heart.

— Psalm 7:10

Yea, the Almighty shall be thy defense.

— Job 22:25

A faithful friend is a strong defense; And he that hath found him hath found a treasure.

— Louisa May Alcott

3

If you are going to college via loans or grants, **make it a priority to have a successful GPA.** If that means taking the minimum number of hours (say, 12), then do that. It's more important to build a solid academic foundation, than it is to feel undue pressure to finish in record time.

In the hearts of all that are wise hearted I have put wisdom.
— Exodus 31:6

Blessed be the name of God forever and ever:
for wisdom and might are his.
— Daniel 2:20

Never regard study as a duty, but as the enviable opportunity
to learn to know the liberating influence of beauty in the
realm of the spirit for your own personal joy and to the profit
of the community to which your later work belongs.

— Albert Einstein

Simple Living

Tip

4

A Rose by Any Other Name Is Still a Rose

There is a story about Abraham Lincoln who was arguing with a political opponent. "How many legs does a cow have?" he asked his adversary.

"Four, of course," came the disgusted reply.

The beginning of wisdom is to call things by their right names.

– Chinese proverb

"That's right," agreed Lincoln. "Now suppose you call the cow's tail a leg; how many legs would the cow have?

"Why, five, of course," was the confident reply.

"Now, that's where you're wrong," said Lincoln. "Calling a cow's tail a leg doesn't make it a leg."

But above all things, my brethren, swear not, neither by heaven, neither by the earth, neither by any other oath: but let your yea be yea; and your nay, nay; lest ye fall into condemnation.
– James 5:12

Simple Living
Tip

5

Never let an opportunity pass to say a kind and encouraging word to or about somebody. Praise good work, regardless of who did it. If criticism is needed, criticize helpfully, never spitefully.

A tree is known by its fruit; a man by his deeds. A good deed is never lost; he who sows courtesy reaps friendship, and he who plants kindness gathers love.

— Saint Basil

And be ye kind one to another, tenderhearted, forgiving one another, even as God for Christ's sake hath forgiven you.
– Ephesians 4:32

Put on then, as God's chosen ones, holy and beloved, compassion, kindness, lowliness, meekness, and patience.
– Colossians 3:12

6

Sometimes, "Fun" Has Consequences

The incredible flight of Larry Walters, a 33-year-old Vietnam veteran and North Hollywood truck driver with no pilot or balloon training, took place on July 2, 1982. Larry filled 45 weather balloons with helium and tethered them in four tiers to an aluminum lawn chair he purchased at Sears for $110, loaded his makeshift aircraft (dubbed the

"Inspiration I") with a large bottle of soda, milk jugs full of water for ballast, a pellet gun, a portable CB radio, an altimeter, and a camera.

Donning a parachute, Larry climbed into his chair from the roof of his girlfriend's home in San Pedro while two friends stood at the ready to untether the craft. He took off a little earlier than expected, however, when his mooring line was cut by the roof's sharp edges. As friends, neighbors, reporters and cameramen looked on, Larry Walters rocketed into the sky above San Pedro. A few minutes later Larry radioed the ground that he was sailing across Los Angeles Harbor toward Long Beach.

Walters had planned to fly 300 miles into the Mojave Desert, but the balloons took him up faster than expected and the wind didn't cooperate, and Walters quickly found himself drifting 16,000 feet above Long Beach. (He later reported that he was "so amazed by the view" that he "didn't even take one picture.") As Larry and his lawn chair drifted into the approach path to Long Beach Municipal Airport, perplexed pilots from two passing Delta and TWA airliners alerted air traffic controllers about what appeared to be an unprotected man floating through the sky in a chair.

Meanwhile, Larry, feeling cold and dizzy in the

thin air three miles above the ground, shot several of his balloons with the pellet gun to bring himself back down to earth. He attempted to aim his descent at a large expanse of grass of a north Long Beach country club, but Larry came up short and ended up entangling his tethers in a set of high-voltage power lines in Long Beach about ten miles from his liftoff site. The plastic tethers protected Walters from electrocution as he dangled above the ground until firemen and utility crews could cut the power to the lines (blacking out a portion of Long Beach for twenty minutes). Larry managed to maneuver his chair over a wall, step out, and cut the chair free.

Larry, who had just set a new altitude record for a flight with gas-filled clustered balloons (although his record was not officially recognized because he had not carried a proper altitude-recording device with him) became an instant celebrity, but the Federal Aviation Administration was not amused. Unable to revoke Walters' pilot's license because he didn't have one, an FAA official announced that they would charge Walters "as soon as we figure out which part [of the FAA code] he violated."

Larry hit the talk show circuit, appearing with Johnny Carson and David Letterman, hosting at a New York bar filled with lawn chairs for the occasion, and receiving an award from the Bonehead Club of Dallas while the FAA pondered his case.

After Walters's hearing before an agency panel, the FAA announced on December 17, 1982 that they were fining him $4,000 for violating four regulations: operating "a civil aircraft for which there is not currently in effect an air-worthiness certificate," creating a collision danger to other aircraft, entering an airport traffic area "without establishing and maintaining two-way communications with the control tower," and failing to take care to prevent hazards to the life and property of others. Larry quickly indicated that he intended to challenge the fines, stating sardonically that if "the FAA was around when the Wright Brothers were testing their aircraft, they would never have been able to make their first flight at Kitty Hawk." He also informed the FAA (and reporters) that he couldn't possibly pay the fine, because he'd put all the money he could save or borrow into his flight.

In April, the FAA signaled their willingness to compromise by dropping one of the charges (they'd decided his lawn chair didn't need an air-worthiness certificate after all) and lowering the fine to $3,000. Walters countered by offering to admit to failing to maintain two-way radio contact with the airport and to pay a $1,000 penalty if the other two charges were dropped. The FAA eventually agreed to accept a $1,500 payment because "the flight was potentially unsafe, but Walters had not intended to endanger anyone."

I will hear what God the LORD will speak: for he will speak peace unto his people, and to his saints: but let them not turn again to folly.
– Psalm 85:8

There are 40 kinds of lunacy, but only one kind of common sense.

— African proverb

Simple Living

Tip

7

Keep skid chains on your tongue:

always say less than you think.

Cultivate a low, persuasive voice. How

you say it often counts more than

what you say.

Kind words do not cost much. Yet they accomplish much.

– Blaise Pascal

*Pleasant words are as an honeycomb, sweet to the soul,
and health to the bones.*
– Proverbs 16:24

A soft answer turneth away wrath.
– Proverbs 15:1

8

Scholarship Tips

Take personal responsibility for getting scholarship aid, and forget about scholarship search services. Many of these services can be scams, and nine times out of ten merely tell you things you can find out yourself. There are thousands of scholarships out there. You just have to be willing to work hard to land one or several.

- http://www.freschinfo.com/search-logon.phtml
- http://www.fastweb.com
- http://www.fastap.org/fastap/index.asp

Start in your hometown. There are plenty of resources. Organizations such as 4H Club, the Jaycees, Lions Club, the Chamber of Commerce, unions, and local businesses frequently offer scholarships. If your parents have local memberships, they may have local scholarship information. Local organizations like to award local scholarships to local candidates.

Always apply for multiple scholarships concurrently. One person actually applied for more than 100 and it paid off! Follow up on the phone with each one, keep application duplicates, and never, ever miss a deadline!

Make yourself into a better scholarship candidate starting your freshman year. If you're involved in extra school, community, hobby, and work activities, you'll have a stronger scholarship application. Remember, don't leave out any of your activities or accomplishments; applications are no place to be humble.

Fill in everything on the application. Be 100 percent accurate and honest in every detail (that includes spelling and grammar).

Tailor each application to the interests of that particular scholarship. This shows that your brain is fully engaged and that you're sincerely interested.

- www.myfuture.com

The scramble to get into college is going to be so terrible in the next few years that students are going to put up with almost anything, even an education.

— Barnaby C. Keeney

Apply thine heart unto instruction, and thine ears to the words of knowledge.
– Proverbs 23:12

9

Be interested in others, their pursuits, their work, their homes and families, Make merry with those who rejoice; with those who weep, mourn. Let everyone you meet, however humble, feel that you regard them as a person of importance.

Never lose sight of the fact that the most important yardstick of your success will be how you treat other people — your family, friends, and coworkers, and even strangers you meet along the way.

– Barbara Bush

Rejoice with them that do rejoice, and weep with them that weep.
– Romans 12:15

For the same cause also do ye joy, and rejoice with me.
– Philippians 2:18

You Can't Please Everyone

A Baptist pastor fresh out of seminary was assigned to a small church in the hills of Kentucky. In his first sermon, he condemned gambling, especially betting on the horses. The sermon was not well received. "You see, Reverend," a parishioner explained, "this whole area is known for its fine horses.

Lots of our members make their living breeding race horses."

The next Sunday the pastor spoke on the evils of smoking, and again, his sermon was not well received — for many of his members also grew tobacco. The third week the pastor preached on the evils of drinking, only to discover after that a major distillery was one of the town's largest employers.

Chastised for his choice of sermon topics, the frustrated pastor exclaimed, "Well, then, what can I preach about?"

A kindly, older woman spoke up and said, "Pastor, preach against those godless Chinese communists. Why, there isn't a Chinese communist within 4,000 miles of here!"

I don't know the key to success, but the key to failure is trying to please everybody.

– Bill Cosby

So, as much as in me is, I am ready to preach the gospel.
– Romans 1:15

Preach the word; be instant in season, out of season; reprove, rebuke, exhort with all longsuffering and doctrine.
– 2 Timothy 4:2

Simple Living

Tip

11

Be cheerful. Don't burden or depress those around you by dwelling on your minor aches and pains and small disappointments. Remember, everyone is carrying some kind of load.

Those who complain most are most to be complained of.

– Matthew Henry

Do all things without murmurings and disputings.
– Philippians 2:14

Why should a living man complain?
– Lamentations 3:39

Simple Living

Tip

12

Keep an open mind. Discuss but don't argue. It is a mark of a superior mind to be able to disagree without being disagreeable.

When one will not quarrel, two cannot.

– Dadi Janki

And the Lord's servant must not be quarrelsome but kindly to
every one, an apt teacher, forbearing.
– 2 Timothy 2:24 (RSV)

Do nothing from selfishness or conceit, but in humility count
others better than yourselves.
– Philippians 2:3 (RSV)

13

Be Honest with Yourself

Believe it or not, this is a true story. Back in 1893, there was a group of four sisters (they called themselves the "Cherry Sisters"), who made their stage debut in Cedar Rapids in a skit they wrote themselves. For three years, the Cherry Sisters performed to packed theaters throughout the Midwest. The crowds were not there because the sisters were greatly talented, however. People came to see them to find out if they were as bad as they had heard. Their unbelievably atrocious acting enraged critics and provoked audiences to throw vegetables at the would-be actresses. Wisely, the sisters thought it best to travel with an iron screen, which they would erect in front of the stage in self-defense.

Amazingly, in 1896 the girls were offered a thousand dollars a week to perform on Broadway — not because they were so good, but because they were so unbelievably bad. Seven years later, after the Cherry Sisters had earned what in that day was a respectable fortune of $200,000, they retired from the stage for the peaceful life back on the farm. Oddly enough, these successful Broadway "stars" remained convinced to the end that they were truly the most talented actresses ever to grace the American stage.[2]

No man was ever so much deceived by another as by himself.

– Greville

Let no man deceive himself.
– 1 Corinthians 3:18

For if a man think himself to be something, when he is nothing, he deceiveth himself.
– Galatians 6:3

14

Let your virtues, if you have any,
speak for themselves. Refuse to talk
of another's vices. Discourage gossip. It
is a waste of valuable time and can be
extremely destructive.

*The measure of people's real character is what they
would do if they knew they would never be found out.*

– J. C. Macauley

*But shun profane and vain babblings: for they will increase
unto more ungodliness.*

– 2 Timothy 2:16

*Pure religion and undefiled before God and the Father is . . . to
keep himself unspotted from the world.*

– James 1:27

15

Be Humble

. . . Richard Daly . . . was mayor of Chicago for 21 years (1955-1976). Mayor Daly was known as a rather formidable guy to work for. One story goes like this. One of Mayor Daly's speechwriters came in and demanded a raise. Mayor Daly responded as could be expected. He said, "I'm not going to give you a raise. You are getting paid more than enough already. It should be enough for you that you are working for a great American hero like myself." And that was the end of it, or so the mayor thought.

Two weeks later, Mayor Daly was on his way to give a speech to a convention of veterans. The speech was going to receive nationwide attention. Now one other thing Mayor Daly was famous for was not reading his speeches until he got up to deliver them. So there he stood before a vast throng of veterans and nationwide press coverage. He began to describe the plight of the veterans. "I'm concerned for you. I have a heart for you. I am deeply convinced that this country needs to take care of its veterans. So, today I am proposing a seventeen point plan that includes the city, state and federal government, to care for the veterans of this country." Now by this time everyone, including Mayor Daly, was on the edge of his seat to hear what the proposal was. He turned the page and saw only these words: "You're on your own now, you great American hero."

I don't know if Daly learned anything at that moment. With his great ego, perhaps he did not. But he should have learned that all of us, no matter how great we think we are, need help.[3]

For I say, through the grace given unto me, to every man
that is among you, not to think of himself more highly
than he ought to think; but to think soberly, according as
God hath dealt to every man the measure of faith.

– Romans 12:3

Our ego is our silent partner — too often
with a controlling interest.

– Cullen Hightower

There's Always Room for Improvement

When Benjamin Franklin was 27 years old, he decided he would take control of his life. He selected 12 virtues he wanted to acquire, and kept a daily chart of his progress in the development of each one. Whenever he missed the mark, he put a black dot beside that virtue. His goal was to ultimately have no dots on the chart.

This method contributed to Franklin's success as an inventor, publisher, and statesman.

*Be ye therefore perfect, even as your Father which is
in heaven is perfect.*
– Matthew 5:48

*Mark the perfect man, and behold the upright: for
the end of that man is peace.*
– Psalm 37:37

*I cannot say whether things will get better if we change; what I
can say is they must change if they are to get better.*

– Georg Christopher Lichtenberg

17

Pay no attention to ill-natured remarks about you. Remember, the person who carried the message may not be the most accurate reporter in the world. Simply live so that no one will believe them.

Live in such a way that you would not be ashamed to sell your parrot to the town gossip.

– Will Rogers

Even a child is known by his doings, whether his work be pure, and whether it be right.

– Proverbs 20:11

Either make the tree good, and his fruit good; or else make the tree corrupt, and his fruit corrupt: for the tree is known by his fruit.

– Matthew 12:33

18

Beware of Those Who Take Advantage of Others

It is said that the city of Frankfort, Kentucky, was enthralled in a big debate many years ago about placing a water fountain in a public square. The argument became heated in the legislature and at the governor's mansion. Finally, a decision was made to ask three contractors to bid on the project.

The first contractor was from Western Kentucky. When asked what his bid was he replied, "Three thousand dollars." Then he was asked to break it down, to which he replied, "A thousand for labor, a thousand for materials, and a thousand for me."

The next contractor was from Eastern Kentucky. When asked to give his bid and to break it down he said, "Six thousand dollars. Two thousand for labor, two thousand for materials, and two thousand for me."

The last contractor was an established contractor from Frankfort who usually got all of the bids for the capital. When asked to give his bid, he replied, "Nine thousand." Then they asked him to break it down.

He closed the doors, looked around cautiously, and then said, "Three thousand for YOU, three thousand for me, and we give the bid to the guy from Western Kentucky!"

A country man between two lawyers is like a fish between two cats.

– Benjamin Franklin

The master commended the dishonest steward for his shrewdness; for the sons of this world are more shrewd in dealing with their own generation than the sons of light.
– Luke 16:8 (RSV)

But Amnon had a friend, whose name was Jonadab . . . and Jonadab was a very crafty man.
– 2 Samuel 13:3 (RSV)

19

Get to Know Others

An old recluse lived in the mountains of Colorado. When he died, distant relatives came from the city to collect his valuables. Upon arriving, all they saw was an old shack with an outhouse beside it. Inside the shack, next to the rock fireplace, was an old cooking pot and his mining equipment. A cracked table with a three-legged chair stood by a tiny window, and a kerosene lamp was on the table. There was a dilapidated cot with a threadbare bedroll on it.

They picked up some of the old relics and started to leave. As they were driving away, an old friend of the recluse, on his mule, flagged them down. "Do you mind if I help myself to what's left in my friend's cabin?" he asked.

"Go right ahead," they replied. After all, they thought, what is inside that shack that could be worth anything?

The old friend entered the shack, and walked directly over to the table. He reached under it, lifting one of the floorboards. He then took out all the gold his friend had discovered over the past 53 years — enough to have built a palace.

The recluse died with only his friend knowing his true worth. As the friend looked out the little window and watched the cloud of dust behind the relatives' car disappear, he said, "They shoulda got to know him better." [4]

You never really know someone until you have been their friend.

– Walker Best

*A friend loveth at all times, and a
brother is born for adversity.*
– Proverbs 17:17

*That I may know him, and the power of his resurrection,
and the fellowship of his sufferings, being made
conformable unto his death.*
– Philippians 3:10

20

When you've done a good job, **don't be too anxious about the credit due.** Do your best, and be patient. Forget about yourself, and let others "remember." Success is much sweeter that way.

The reward for work well done is the opportunity to do more.

– Jonas Salk

His lord said unto him, Well done, thou good and faithful servant: thou hast been faithful over a few things, I will make thee ruler over many things: enter thou into the joy of thy lord.
– Matthew 25:21

And in every work that he began in the service of the house of God, and in the law, and in the commandments, to seek his God, he did it with all his heart, and prospered.
– 2 Chronicles 31:21

21

Recognize Danger

Iron Eyes Cody was an actor who once did a TV spot for the "Keep America Beautiful" campaign. He was an Indian drifting alone in a canoe. As he saw how our waters are being polluted, a single tear rolled down his cheek, telling the whole story. This powerful public service commercial still shows up on TV screens thirty years later.

In 1988, Cody repeated an old Indian legend in Guideposts magazine:

Many years ago, Indian youths would go away in solitude to prepare for manhood. One such youth hiked into a beautiful valley, green with trees, bright with flowers. There he fasted. But on the third day, as he looked up at the surrounding mountains, he noticed one tall rugged peak, capped with dazzling snow. I will test myself against that mountain, he thought. He put on his buffalo-hide shirt, threw his blanket over his shoulders and set off to climb the peak. When he reached the top he stood on the rim of the world. He could see forever, and his heart swelled with pride. Then he heard a rustle at his feet, and looking down, he saw a snake. Before he could move, the snake spoke.

"I am about to die," said the snake. "It is too cold for me up here and I am freezing. There is no food and I am starving. Put me under your shirt and take me down to the valley."

"No," said the youth. "I am forewarned. I know your kind. You are a rattlesnake. If I pick you up, you will bite, and your bite will kill me."

"Not so," said the snake. "I will treat you differently. If you do this for me, you will be special. I will not harm you."

The youth resisted awhile, but this was a very

persuasive snake with beautiful markings. At last the youth tucked it under his shirt and carried it down to the valley. There he laid it gently on the grass, when suddenly the snake coiled, rattled, and leapt, biting him on the leg.

"But you promised…" cried the youth.

"You knew what I was when you picked me up." said the snake as it slithered away.

Abstain from all appearance of evil.
– 1 Thessalonians. 5:22

We sin two kinds of sin. We sin one kind of sin as though we trip off the curb, and it overtakes us by surprise. We sin a second kind of sin when we deliberately set ourselves up to fall.

– Francis Schaeffer

Set Proper Priorities

A young boy by the name of James had a desire to be the most famous manufacturer and salesman of cheese in the world. He planned on becoming rich and famous by making and selling cheese and began with a little buggy pulled by a pony named Paddy. After making his cheese, he would load his wagon and he and Paddy would drive down the streets of Chicago to sell the cheese. As the months passed, the young boy began to despair because he was not making any money, in spite of his long hours and hard work.

One day he pulled his pony to a stop and began to talk to him. He said, "Paddy, there is something wrong. We are not doing it right. I am afraid we have things turned around and our priorities are not where they ought to be. Maybe we ought to serve God and place him first in our lives." The boy drove home and made a covenant that for the rest of his life he would first serve God and then would work as God directed.

Many years after this, the young boy, now a man, stood as Sunday school superintendent at North Shore

Baptist Church in Chicago and said, "I would rather be a layman in the North Shore Baptist Church than to head the greatest corporation in America. My first job is serving Jesus."

So, every time you take a take a bite of Philadelphia cream cheese, sip a cup of Maxwell House, mix a quart of Kool-Aid, slice up a DiGiorno pizza, cook a pot of macaroni & cheese, spread some Grey Poupon, stir a bowl of Cream of Wheat, slurp down some Jell-O, eat the cream out of the middle of an Oreo cookie, or serve some Stove Top, remember a boy, his pony named Paddy, and the promise little James L. Kraft made to serve God and work as He directed.[5]

I had rather be a doorkeeper in the house of my God, than to dwell in the tents of wickedness.

– Psalm 84:10

This book of the law shall not depart out of thy mouth; but thou shalt meditate therein day and night, that thou mayest observe to do according to all that is written therein: for then thou shalt make thy way prosperous, and then thou shalt have good success.

– Joshua 1:8

You don't have to lie awake nights to succeed — just stay awake days.

– Anonymous

Simple Living

Tip

23

Take the time to attend church

services at least once a week. If not

Sunday, pick Wednesday — or a Bible

study the other nights of the week.

Every time I pass a church
I stop in for a visit,
So when I'm carried home one day
The Lord won't say, "Who is it?"

– Anonymous

Not forsaking the assembling of ourselves together, as the manner of some is; but exhorting one another: and so much the more, as ye see the day approaching.

– Hebrews 10:25

For where two or three are gathered together in my name, there am I in the midst of them.

– Matthew 18:20

24

Develop a Work Ethic

December 24, 1848

Dear Johnston:

Your request for 80 dollars, I do not think it best to comply with now. At the various times when I have helped you a little, you have said to me, "We can get along very well now," but in a very short time I find you in the same difficulty again. Now this can only happen by some defect in your conduct. What that defect is, I think I know. You are not lazy, and still you are an idler. I doubt whether since I saw you, you have done a good whole day's work, in any one day. You do not very much dislike to work, and still you do not work much, merely because it does not seem to you that you could get much for it.

This habit of uselessly wasting time, is the whole difficulty; it is vastly important to you, and still more so to your children, that you should break this habit. It is more important to them, because they have longer to live, and can keep out of an idle habit before they are in it, easier than they can get out after they are in.

You are now in need of some ready money; and

what I propose is, that you shall go to work, "tooth and nail," for somebody who will give you money for it.

Let Father and your boys take charge of your things at home — prepare for a crop, and make the crop, and you go to work for the best money wages, or in discharge of any debt you owe, that you can get. And to secure you a fair reward for your labor, I now promise you that for every dollar you will, between this and the first of May, get for your own labor either in money or in your own indebtedness, I will then give you one other dollar.

By this, if you hire yourself at ten dollars a month, from me you will get ten more, making twenty dollars a month for your work. In this, I do not mean you shall go off to St. Louis, or the lead mines, or the gold mines in California, but I mean for you to go at it for the best wages you can get close to home — in Coles County.

Now if you will do this, you will soon be out of debt, and what is better, you will have a habit that will keep you from getting in debt again. But if I should now clear you out, next year you will be just as deep in as ever. You say you would almost give your place in Heaven for $70 or $80. Then you value your place in Heaven very cheaply, for I am sure you can with the offer I make you get the $70 or $80 for four or five months' work. You say if I furnish you the money you will deed me the land, and if you don't pay the money back, you will deliver possession.

    Nonsense! If you can't now live with the land, how will you then live without it? You have always been kind to me, and I do not now mean to be unkind to you. On the contrary, if you will but follow my advice, you will find it worth more than eight times 80 dollars to you.

                    Affectionately

                    Your brother,

                    A. Lincoln

The desire of the slothful killeth him; for his hands refuse to labour.
– Proverbs 21:25

Happiness, I have discovered, is nearly always a rebound from hard work.

– David Grayson

Simple Living

Tip

25

If you are a disorganized person, and feel that you're drowning in classwork, **take care of a housekeeping matter:** do all your laundry. Clean your dorm room. Tidy up the apartment. Detail your car. Eliminating physical clutter is a wonderful path to eliminating mental clutter.

It strikes at a fundamental human need to be organized.

– Donna Dubinsky

Thus saith the LORD, Set thine house in order.
– 2 Kings 20:1

Let all things be done decently and in order.
– 1 Corinthians 14:40

26

Be Gracious

A number of years ago, *Newsweek* magazine carried the story of the memorial service held for Hubert Humphrey, former vice-president of the United States. Hundreds of people came from all over the world to say good-bye to their old friend and colleague.

But one person who came was shunned and ignored by virtually everyone there. Nobody would look at him, much less speak to him. That person was former President Richard Nixon. Not long before, he had gone through the shame and infamy of Watergate. He was back in Washington for the first time since his resignation from the presidency.

Then a very special thing happened, perhaps the only thing that could have made a difference and broken the ice. President Jimmy Carter, who was in the White House at that time, came into the room. Before he was seated, he saw Nixon over against the wall, all by himself. He went over to [him] as though he were greeting a family member, stuck out his hand to the former president, and smiled broadly. To the surprise of everyone there, the two of them embraced each other, and Carter said, "Welcome home, Mr. President! Welcome home!"

Commenting on that, *Newsweek* magazine asserted, "If there was a turning point in Nixon's long ordeal in the wilderness, it was that moment and that gesture of love and compassion."[6]

There is no friend like an old friend who has shared our morning days, no greeting like his welcome, no homage like his praise.

– Oliver Wendell Holmes, Jr.

Therefore all things whatsoever ye would that men should do to you, do ye even so to them: for this is the law and the prophets.
– Matthew 7:12

And of his fullness have all we received, and grace for grace.
– John 1:16

Simple Living

Tip

27

If you are an organized person, and you begin to feel confined by the routine of school, study, and test taking . . . **do something frivolous.** Go see a movie. Feed the ducks. Play darts. Rigidity isn't good for anyone; loosen up!

Be careless in your dress if you will, but keep a tidy soul.

– Mark Twain

Let a little water, I pray you, be fetched, and wash your feet, and rest yourselves under the tree.

– Genesis 18:4

His soul shall dwell at ease; and his seed shall inherit the earth.

– Psalm 25:13

Simple Living

Tip

28

J. D. Rockefeller's 3 Simple Rules for

Anyone Who Wants to Become Rich:

Go to work early.

Stay at work late.

Find oil.

Early to rise and early to bed makes a
male healthy, wealthy . . . and dead.

– James Thurber

And ye shall rise up early.
– Genesis 19:2

He also that is slothful in his work is brother to him that is a great waster.
– Proverbs 18:9

Tip

29

Be Clever

Old aunts used to come up to me at weddings, poking me in the ribs and cackling, telling me, "You're next." They stopped after I started doing the same thing to them at funerals.

I don't think much of a man who is not wiser today than he was yesterday.

– Abraham Lincoln

Be wise now therefore.
– Psalm 2:10

*Hear thou, my son, and be wise, and guide
thine heart in the way.*
– Proverbs 23:19

30

Take Time to Make Time

One man challenged another to an all-day wood chopping contest. The challenger worked very hard, stopping only for a brief lunch break. The other man had a leisurely lunch and took several breaks during the day. At the end of the day, the challenger was surprised and annoyed to find that the other fellow had chopped substantially more wood than he had.

"I don't get it," he said. "Every time I checked, you were taking a rest, yet you chopped more wood than I did."

"But you didn't notice," said the winning woodsman, "that I was sharpening my ax when I sat down to rest." [7]

See then that ye walk circumspectly, not as fools, but as wise,
Redeeming the time, because the days are evil.
– Ephesians 5:15-16

The ability to concentrate and use time well is everything.

– Lee Iacocca

Simple Living

Tip

31

Daily pray for those you come in contact with, especially those people who are difficult to deal with. You will be surprised at the change this will bring.

There is nothing that makes us love a man so much as praying for him.

– William Law

But I say unto you, Love your enemies, bless them that curse you, do good to them that hate you, and pray for them which despitefully use you, and persecute you. —
– Matthew 5:44

Moreover as for me, God forbid that I should sin against the LORD in ceasing to pray for you.
– 1 Samuel 12:23

Tip

32

Be Quick on Your Feet

Paul got off the elevator on the 40th floor and nervously knocked on his blind date's door. She opened it and was as beautiful and charming as everyone had said.

"I'll be ready in a few minutes," she said. "Why don't you play with Rollo while you're waiting? He does wonderful tricks. He rolls over, shakes hands, sits up, and if you make a hoop with your arms, he'll jump through."

The dog followed Paul onto the balcony and started rolling over. Paul made a hoop with his arms and Rollo jumped through — and over the balcony railing. Just then Paul's date walked out.

"Isn't Rollo the cutest, happiest dog you've ever seen?"

"To tell the the truth," he replied, "he seemed a little depressed to me."

I do not feel obliged to believe that that same God who has endowed us with sense, reason, and intellect has intended us to forego their use.

– Galileo Galilei

Keep Yourself Busy

Unamuno, the Spanish philosopher, tells about the Roman aqueduct at Segovia, in his native Spain. It was built in 109 A.D. For eighteen hundred years, it carried cool water from the mountains to the hot and thirsty city. Nearly sixty generations of men drank from its flow. Then came another generation, a recent one, who said, "This aqueduct is so great a marvel that it ought to be preserved fo our children, as a museum piece. We shall relieve it of its centuries-long labor."

They did; they laid modern iron pipes. They gave the ancient bricks and mortar a reverent rest. And what happened to the aqueduct? It began to fall apart. The sun beating on the dry mortar caused it to crumble. The bricks and stone sagged and threatened to fall. What ages of service could not destroy, idleness disintegrated.[8]

Slothfulness casteth into a deep sleep; and an idle soul shall suffer hunger.
– Proverbs 19:15

You can't teach people to be lazy — either they have it, or they don't.
– Dagwood Bumstead

Chickens Sometimes Come Home to Roost

The rules at a particular university were such that if the professor were not present in the classroom by 15 minutes past the hour, the class was considered a "walk" and the students were free to leave — with no penalties for missing a class.

The rooms were equipped with the type of wall clocks that "jumped" ahead each minute, in a very noticeable fashion. As it were, these clocks were also not of the most sophisticated construction. Some enterprising student discovered that if one were to hit the clock with chalkboard erasers, it would cause the clock to "jump" ahead 1 minute.

So, it became almost daily practice for these students to take target practice at the clock (as it would have it, this particular professor was not the most punctual, and the students considered him severely "absent-minded"). A few well aimed erasers, and lo, 15 minutes were passed, and class dismissed itself.

Well, when the day for the next exam rolled

around, the professor strolled into the room, passed out the exams, and told them, "You have one hour to complete."

The professor then proceeded to collect the erasers from around the room, and gleefully took aim at the clock. When he had successfully "jumped" the clock forward one hour, he closed the class and collected the exam papers.

Life does teach some lessons the hard way.

Behold, ye have sinned against the LORD:
and be sure your sin will find you out.
– Numbers 32:23

And I will recompense them according to their deeds,
and according to the works of their own hand.
– Jeremiah 25:14

Happy shall he be, that rewardeth thee
as thou hast served us.
– Psalm 137:8

Do something nice for someone and for yourself at the same time. Maybe you have tickets to the big game or the theater. Give one to a fellow student who just happens to be a whiz in chemistry. Trade a ticket for a tutorial session.

*And as ye would that men should do to you, do ye
also to them likewise.*
– Luke 6:31

And be ye kind one to another.
– Ephesians 4:32

As they did unto me, so have I done unto them.
– Judges 15:11

Don't cheat! Studies show that as many as 65 percent of American students cheat on tests, on homework, anywhere they can. And let's be honest: cheating is just plain wrong, but it packs a double-whammy: you can get caught! Is cheating on a test worth telling your dad, "Oh, by the way, I've been expelled"?

The just man walketh in his integrity.

– Proverbs 20:7

He that is faithful in that which is least is faithful also in much.

– Luke 16:10

I went to New York University and I was thrown out of NYU my freshman year for cheating on my metaphysics final. I looked within the soul of the boy sitting next to me.

– Woody Allen

Always Be Willing to Help

A rat looked through a crack in the wall to see the farmer and his wife opening a package. What food might it contain? He was aghast to discover that it was a rat trap. Retreating to the farmyard, the rat proclaimed the warning, "There is a rat trap in the house, a rat trap in the house!"

The chicken clucked and scratched, raised her head and said, "Excuse me,

Mr. Rat, I can tell this is a grave concern to you, but it is of no consequence to me. I cannot be bothered by it."

The rat turned to the pig and told him, "There is a rat trap in the house, a rat trap in the house!"

"I am so very sorry Mr. Rat," sympathized the pig, "but there is nothing I can do about it but pray. Be assured that you are in my prayers."

The rat turned to the cow. She said, "Like wow, Mr. Rat. A rat trap. I am in grave danger. Duh?"

So the rat returned to the house, head down and dejected, to face the farmer's rat trap alone. That very night a sound was heard throughout the house, like the sound of a rat trap catching its prey.

The farmer's wife rushed to see what was caught. In the darkness, she did not see that it was a venomous snake whose tail the trap had caught. The snake bit the farmer's wife. The farmer rushed her to the hospital.

She returned home with a fever. Now, everyone knows you treat a fever with fresh chicken soup, so the farmer took his hatchet to the farmyard for the soup's main ingredient.

His wife's sickness continued so that friends and neighbors came to sit with her around the clock. To feed them, the farmer butchered the pig.

The farmer's wife did not get well. She died, and so many people came for her funeral that the farmer had the cow slaughtered to provide meat for all of them to eat.

So, the next time you hear that someone is facing a problem and think that it does not concern you, remember that when there is a rat trap in the house, the whole farmyard is at risk.

Look not every man on his own things, but every man also on the things of others.
– Philippians 2:4

Christianity demands a level of caring that transcends human inclinations.

– Erwin Lutzer

38

Pay close attention to your friends. If you have to go to extremes, change your surroundings, anything to get away from the wrong crowd. The alternative is to watch your grades (and future) go south. For this short-term fun, you'll sacrifice the next 50 years.

The man who follows the crowd will usually get no further than the crowd.

– Alan Ashley-Pitt

He that walketh with wise men shall be wise: but a companion of fools shall be destroyed.

– Proverbs 13:20

Be not deceived: evil communications corrupt good manners.

– 1 Corinthians 15:33

Learn Who Your Neighbors Are

A man asked Jesus, "And who is my neighbor?"

Jesus answered, "A certain man went down from Jerusalem to Jericho, and fell among thieves, who stripped him of his raiment, and wounded him, and departed, leaving him half dead.

"By chance, there came down a certain priest that way: and when he saw him, he passed by on the other side.

"Also, a Levite, when he was at the place, came and looked on him, and passed by on the other side.

"Then a certain Samaritan, as he journeyed, came where he was, and when he saw him, he had compassion on him, and went to him, binding up his wounds, pouring in oil and wine. He set him on his own beast, and brought him to an inn, and took care of him.

"The next day, when he departed, he took out two pence, and gave them to the host, and said unto him, Take care of him; and whatever you spend more, when I come again, I will repay thee.

"Which now of these three, do you think, was a neighbor unto him that fell among the thieves?"

The man said, "He that showed mercy on him."

Then said Jesus unto him, "Go, and do thou likewise."

> – from Luke 10

The impersonal hand of government can never replace the helping hand of a neighbor.

– Hubert H. Humphrey

*For I have given you an example, that ye
should do as I have done to you.*
– John 13:15

*Now the God of patience and consolation
grant you to be likeminded one toward
another according to Christ Jesus.*
– Romans 15:5

Here's something that will just make you feel good. **Help out a fellow student,** and do it quietly. Find that person who is shy and self-reliant... and treat him to a nice meal. Give someone a ride to a ballgame. Help a new student find their classes. Share your notes with someone who missed class. Help a sick friend to know what they missed in class. The gesture will be appreciated, and you never know when a "random act of kindness" will be the trigger to someone's future.

And walk in love, as Christ also hath loved us.
– Ephesians 5:2

And the Lord make you to increase and abound in love one toward another.
– 1 Thessalonians 3:12

Live for something. Do good, and leave behind you a monument of virtue that the storms of time can never destroy. Write your name in kindness, love, and mercy on the hearts of thousands you come in contact with year by year, and you will never be forgotten. Your name and your good deeds will shine as the stars of heaven.

– Thomas Chalmers

40

Set realistic goals, and do your homework. Do you make good grades, but do you also want to, say, play someday in the NBA? Find out how many men play college basketball, then find out how many go on to be professionals in the sport. Are your goals realistic? Think as objectively as possible: do you have the physical ability to do this, to play beyond high school or college? If so, go for it. But having a set goal is the key.

Seek ye first the kingdom of God, and His righteousness.
– Matthew 6:33

*Walk worthy of God, who hath called you unto
His kingdom and glory.*
– 1 Thessalonians 2:12

*In life, as in football, you don't go far unless
you know where the goalposts are.*

– Arnold H. Glasgow

41

Be Careful What You Cherish

Many analogies can be drawn from God's creation, and the story of the butterfly named "Maculinea Arion" is most instructive.

As an adult, the butterfly lays its eggs on a plant, and the eggs hatch later. After feeding on the plant for several weeks, a young caterpillar will make its way to the ground. In order to complete its development, it must meet a certain kind of ant.

When such an ant meets the caterpillar, the ant strokes it with its antennae, and the caterpillar exudes a sweet fluid from a special gland on its tenth segment. Apparently the ant likes this substance, because it then carries the caterpillar home to its nest.

There, the ants drink the sweet fluid exuded by the caterpillar. The ants show their appreciation to the caterpillar by letting him spend the winter in a special cavity of their nest. And, what does the caterpillar eat? The baby ants. It continues to eat the young ants until spring. Eventually it emerges as an adult butterfly and flies away to establish more of its kind, and the cycle starts all over again.

Some people are not much different from the ants. For you see, they cherish a luxury item to the injury of themselves.[9]

We are not punished for our sins, but by them.

– Elbert Hubbard

Let us lay aside every weight, and the sin which doth so easily beset us, and let us run with patience the race that is set before us.
– Hebrews 12:1

A man is first startled by sin; then it becomes pleasing, then easy, then delightful, then frequent, then habitual, then confirmed. The man is impenitent, then obstinate, and then he is damned.

– Jeremy Taylor

42

This is an obvious one, but so important. As a student, you are devoting some time to studying. So, do two things that will dramatically help: **get plenty of sleep** (try going to bed no later than ten o'clock on weeknights) AND **eliminate sugar** as much as possible from your diet. These two things will boost your energy so much, you'll be surprised.

In peace I will both lie down and sleep; for thou alone, O LORD,
makest me dwell in safety.
– Psalm 4:8 (RSV)

Come unto me, all ye that labour and are heavy laden, and I
will give you rest.
– Matthew 11:28

Sleep recreates. The Bible indicates that sleep is not meant only for
the recuperation of a man's body, but that there is a tremendous
furtherance of spiritual and moral life during sleep.

– Oswald Chambers

43

Struggling with math? If you're trying and still seeing your grade disappear from sight, openly **talk about it** with your instructor. Math teachers are usually more than willing to share insights and will be glad to go over formulas, etc. Failing math is an option you can choose to refuse!

If you are struggling with a difficult subject, say, English, try this: instead of forcing yourself to read a Shakespeare play, attend one. **Think visual.** Often, an obstacle like this can be remedied by the stimulation of watching actors and colorful sets on a stage. It can broaden your horizons.

And be renewed in the spirit of your mind.
– Ephesians 4:23

And here is the mind which hath wisdom.
– Revelation 17:9

No man was ever so much deceived by another as by himself.

– Greville

Rules for Teenagers

1. Life is not fair. Get used to it. The average teenager uses the phrase "It's not fair" 8.6 times a day. You got it from your parents, who said it so often you decided they must be the most idealistic generation ever. When they started hearing it from their own kids, they realized Rule No. 1.

2. The real world won't care as much about your self-esteem as your

school does. It'll expect you to accomplish something before you feel good about yourself. This may come as a shock. Usually, when inflated self-esteem meets reality, kids complain that it's not fair. (See rule 1.)

3. Sorry, you won't make $40,000 a year right out of high school. And you won't be a vice president or have a car phone either. You may even have to wear a uniform that doesn't have a GAP label.

4. If you think your teacher is tough, wait 'til you get a boss. He doesn't have tenure, so he tends to be a bit edgier. When you screw up, he's not going to ask you how you feel about it.

5. Flipping burgers is not beneath your dignity. Your grandparents had a different word for burger flipping. They called it opportunity. They weren't embarrassed making minimum wage either. . . .

6. It's not your parents' fault. If you screw up, you are responsible. This is the flip side of "It's my life," and "You're not the boss of me," and other eloquent proclamations of your generation. When you turn 18, it's on your dime. Don't whine about it, or you'll sound like a baby boomer.

7. Before you were born your parents weren't as boring as they are now. They got that way paying your bills, cleaning up your room, and listening to you tell them how idealistic you are. . . .

8. Your school may have done away with winners and losers — life hasn't. In some schools, they'll give you as many times as you want to get the right answer. Failing grades have been abolished and class valedictorians scrapped, lest anyone's feelings be hurt. Effort is as important as results. This, of course, bears not the slightest resemblance to anything in real life. (See rules 1, 2, and 4.)

9. Life is not divided into semesters, and you don't get summers off. Not even Easter break. They expect you to show up every day. For eight hours. And you don't get a new life every ten weeks. It just goes on and on. While we're at it, very few jobs are interested in fostering your self-expression or helping you find yourself. Fewer still lead to self-realization. (See rules 1 and 2.)

10. Television is not real life. Your life is not a sitcom. Your problems will not all be solved in 30 minutes, minus time for commercials. In real life, people actually have to leave the coffee shop to go to jobs. . . .

11. Be nice to nerds. You may end up working for them. We all could.

12. Smoking does not make you look cool. It makes you look moronic. Next time you're out cruising, watch an 11-year-old with a butt in his mouth. That's what you look like to anyone over 20. Ditto for "expressing yourself" with purple hair and/or pierced body parts.

13. You are not immortal. (See rule 12.) If you are under the impression that living fast, dying young and leaving a beautiful corpse is romantic, you obviously haven't seen one of your peers at room temperature lately.

14. Enjoy this while you can. Sure parents are a pain, school's a bother, and life is depressing. But someday you'll realize how wonderful it was to be a kid. Maybe you should start now. You're welcome.[10]

> *We make a living by what we get,*
> *we make a life by what we give.*
>
> – Sir Winston Churchill

45

Do you have a roommate who's driving you nuts? Rather than dig-in and wait-out that person, choose to move out. **Take the initiative.** It will save both of you — especially YOU — some bitterness and strife.

You must first get along with yourself before you can get along with others.

– Anthony J. D'Angelo

Can two walk together, except they be agreed?
– Amos 3:3

I therefore, a prisoner for the Lord, beg you to lead a life worthy of the calling to which you have been called, with all lowliness and meekness, with patience, forbearing one another in love, eager to maintain the unity of the Spirit in the bond of peace.
– Ephesians 4:1-3

46

Failure Is Not Fatal

By 1989, baseball player Nolan
Ryan reached an incredible 5,000
strikeouts, and all those no hitters.
Ryan was a phenomenal baseball
player.

In Ryan's rookie year, 18 years
earlier, Gil Hodges had been the
manager of the Mets, and was
impatient with Ryan. Although Ryan
could consistently throw the ball over

ninety miles an hour, most of the time it didn't go over the plate. He was walking everybody and hitting a lot of people, too. Hodges told Ryan at the beginning of a particular game that he would have to pitch better in that game or he would pull him out and trade him. He would be finished.

Ryan went into that game trying to do his best, determined that he was going to succeed. He was miserable. He walked something like seven or eight batters in four innings. Hodges took him out.

After the game, Richard Reeves went down into the locker room to interview the players. He noticed Nolan Ryan was apart from the others, looking into a mirror, obviously having difficulty tying his tie. Reeves got closer to him and noticed that there were tears in his eyes. He was crying. He couldn't see to tie his tie. Later that season, Ryan was traded to the Angels.

Reeves remembered that incident on the occasion of celebrating Nolan Ryan as one of the immortals of baseball. He remembered that this legendary man, Nolan Ryan, began thinking he had failed. But he kept on working. He kept on practicing. He kept on doing his job.

Many that are first shall be last; and the last shall be first.
– Mark 10:31

Unto whomsoever much is given, of him shall be much required.
– Luke 12:48

Failing doesn't make you a failure. Giving up, accepting your failure, refusing to try again does!

– Richard Exely

Are you having a personality clash with a teacher? Do this: schedule an appointment with him or her, and prepare ahead of time. Go over your concerns on note cards and practice, if necessary. Then meet with the teacher. By **acting like an adult** (and refraining from gossiping about your teacher, or worse, going over his or her head), you will show yourself worthy of a rational discussion of the problems. Remember: conflict resolution works!

Moreover if thy brother shall trespass against thee, go and tell him his fault between thee and him alone: if he shall hear thee, thou hast gained thy brother.
– Matthew 18:15

Argue your case with your neighbor himself, and do not disclose another's secret.
– Proverbs 25:9

All the problems of the world could be settled if people were only willing to think. The trouble is that people very often resort to all sorts of devices in order not to think, because thinking is such hard work.

– Thomas John Watson, Sr

48

Forgive and Forget

In his book, *Lee: The Last Years,*
Charles Bracelen Flood reports that
after the Civil War, Robert E. Lee visited
a Kentucky lady who took him to the
remains of a grand old tree in front of
her house. There she bitterly cried that its
limbs and trunk had been destroyed by
Federal artillery fire. She looked to Lee for
a word condemning the North or at least
sympathizing with her loss.

After a brief silence, Lee said, "Cut it down, my dear madam, and forget it."

It is better to forgive the injustices of the past than to allow them to remain, let bitterness take root, and poison the rest of our life.[11]

Then came Peter to him, and said, Lord, how oft shall my brother sin against me, and I forgive him? till seven times? Jesus saith unto him, I say not unto thee, Until seven times: but, Until seventy times seven.
– Matthew 18:21-22

Forgiveness is an act of the will, and the will can function regardless of the temperature of the heart.

– Corrie Ten Boom

Be Happy with What You Have

Leo Tolstoy once wrote a story about a successful peasant farmer who was not satisfied with his lot. He wanted more of everything. One day he received a novel offer. For 1,000 rubles, he could buy all the land he could walk around in a day. The only catch in the deal was that he had to be back at his starting point by sundown.

Early the next morning he started

out walking at a fast pace. By midday he was very tired, but he kept going, covering more and more ground. Well into the afternoon he realized that his greed had taken him far from the starting point. He quickened his pace and as the sun began to sink low in the sky, he began to run, knowing that if he did not make it back by sundown the opportunity to become an even bigger landholder would be lost.

As the sun began to sink below the horizon he came within sight of the finish line. Gasping for breath, his heart pounding, he called upon every bit of strength left in his body and staggered across the line just before the sun disappeared. He immediately collapsed, blood streaming from his mouth. In a few minutes he was dead. Afterward, his servants dug a grave, not much over six feet long and three feet wide. The title of Tolstoy's story was "How Much Land Does a Man Need?"[12]

You can't have everything; where would you put it?

– Anonymous

For the man who has everything: a calendar to tell him when his payments are due.

– Anonymous

For I have learned, in whatsoever state I am,
therewith to be content.
– Philippians 4:11

Tip

50

Be Grateful

Pastor Victor Shepherd tells about being in the audience when a missionary surgeon was speaking to a small group of university students about his work in the Gaza Strip. "He was telling us that we North American 'fat cats' knew nothing about gratitude. Nothing!

"On one occasion he had stopped

at by a peasant hovel to see a woman on whom he had performed surgery. She and her husband were dirt poor. Their livestock supply consisted of one Angora rabbit and two chickens. For income, the woman combed the hair out of the rabbit, spun the hair into yarn and sold it. For food, she and her husband ate the eggs from the chickens. The woman insisted that the missionary surgeon stay for lunch. He accepted the invitation and said he would be back for lunch after he had gone down the road to see another postoperative patient.

"An hour and a half later he was back. He peeked

into the cooking pot to see what he was going to eat. He saw one rabbit and two chickens. The woman had given up her entire livestock supply — her income, her food, everything. He concluded his story by reminding us that we knew nothing of gratitude. He wept unashamedly. The incident will stay with me forever."[13]

For today and its blessings, I owe the world an attitude of gratitude.

– Clarence E. Hodges

Enter into his gates with thanksgiving, and into his courts with praise: be thankful unto him, and bless his name.
– Psalm 100:4

Bless the LORD, O my soul, and forget not all his benefits.
– Psalm 103:2

51

Encourage Others

A group of frogs were traveling through the woods, and two of them fell into a deep pit. All the other frogs gathered around the pit. When they saw how deep the pit was, they told the two frogs that they were as good as dead. The two frogs ignored the comments and tried to jump up out of the pit with all of their might. The other frogs kept telling them to stop, that they were as good as dead.

Finally, one of the frogs took heed to what the other frogs were saying and gave up. He fell down and died. The other frog continued to jump as hard as he could. Once again, the crowd of frogs yelled at him to stop the pain and just die. He jumped even harder and finally made it out.

When he got out, the other frogs said, "Did you not hear us?" The frog explained to them that he was deaf. He thought they were encouraging him the entire time.

This story teaches two lessons:

1. There is power of life and death in the tongue. An encouraging word to someone who is down can lift them up and help them make it through the day.

2. A destructive word to someone who is down can be what it takes to kill them. Be careful of what you say. Speak life to those who cross your path. The power of words . . . it is sometimes hard to understand that an encouraging word can go such a long way. Anyone can speak words that tend to rob another of the spirit to continue in difficult times.

Special is the individual who will take the time to encourage another.

He climbs highest who helps another up.

– Zig Ziglar

Therefore I thought it necessary to exhort the brethren.
– 2 Corinthians 9:5

The LORD is my light and my salvation; whom shall I fear? the LORD is the strength of my life; of whom shall I be afraid?
– Psalm 27:1

Simple Living
References

[1] *Homelife* magazine.

[2] from www.devotions.net.

[3] Story taken from: *Journey Toward God: New Community Small Group Study on Exodus* (Zondervan), p.33.

[4] "Honey from the Bee Hive" vol. 5, no. 2, July-Sept. 2001, quoting and adapted from "The VaryIdea Ministry Ideas," June 1998.

[5] Adapted by Brett Blair from Michael Green, *Illustrations for Biblical Preaching*, Baker, p. 331.

[6] As told by Maxie Dunnam in *The Workbook on Living as a Christian*, pp. 112-113

[7] L. S. Chafer, *Grace*.

[8] *Resource*, Sept/Oct, 1992, p. 4.

[9] Michael Green, *Illustrations For Biblical Preaching*, Grand Rapids: Baker, 1989, p. 238, adapted.

[10] Charles J. Sykes, *Dumbing Down Our Kids: Why American Children Feel Good About Themselves But Can't Read, Write, Or Add.*

[11] Michael Williams, *Leadership*, vol. 5, no. 4.

[12] *Bits and Pieces*, November 1991.

[13] from "Priortizing Our Responsibilities," a sermon by Rev. John P. Wood.

Simple Living
Photo Credits